NIA'S SUMMER VACATION IN
THE CARIBBEAN

Danielle Fairbairn-Bland

Made 2 Heal

New York, NY

ISBN: 978-1-7367094-8-1

For more books, visit us online at www.deefbland.com or email info@deefbland.com

This book is dedicated to
my Grandparents, Arleigh & Clarette
Douglas and the priceless memories at
our family home in Kingstown Park,
SVG. May these memories live forever
and bind us together with cords that
can never be broken.

Today is Nia's last day of the school year! Every summer she visits her Gran-Gran and family on the beautiful island of St. Vincent. Nia thinks about everything she will need for the summer. She's almost ready to go, but she needs to pack a few more things.

Last month, Nia and her mom packed a huge, blue plastic shipping barrel with special gifts for aunts, uncles, and cousins.

c/o
Gran Gran
Douglas
Kingstown Park
St. Vincent

The best part was when Nia climbed to the top of the barrel, twirled twice, and jumped three times to help Mom tightly close the barrel. Mom shipped the barrel so it will arrive when Nia is in St. Vincent and can watch her family's excitement when they unpack it.

On the day of the trip, Nia wakes up extra early to get ready before leaving for the airport. Nia says goodbye to New York City – the trains, the busy streets, the bright lights. "New York, I will miss you, but I will be back again!" she says.

"To Gran-Gran's house I go," she says. She looks forward to the warm weather, the beaches, and the fresh fruit. Most of all, Nia can't wait to spend quality time with her Gran-Gran and family on the island.

Nia has to first board a really big plane that takes her from New York all the way to Trinidad. Then, she takes a tiny plane that flies above the water and under the clouds for 54 minutes. After waking up from a long nap, Nia hears the pilot say, "Welcome to Paradise, the land of the blessed. The current temperature is 95 degrees in the shade."

Everyone on the plane claps and shouts with praise, lifting their hands in celebration. Nia is bursting with joy. "Let the fun begin!" she says.

The sweet sound of steel pan fills the air, and the warm breeze gently blows through her hair as she walks away from the plane. Nia's passport is stamped, and she picks up her suitcase. "Home sweet home!" Nia exclaims.

Nia is greeted by so many members of her family: Gran-Gran, Grandfather, aunts, uncles, and cousins. She gets tight hugs and kisses from everyone! Nia is overjoyed to see their familiar faces.

"Welcome home, Nia!" her family shouts with glee. She feels like a Caribbean princess.

We are Family.   Family is Love.

Family is Joy.   Family is Laughter.

Family is Fun.   Family is Everything.

To get to Gran-Gran's house, they drive up and down, and around and around hilltops and mountainsides. Nia sees coconut trees, hibiscus flowers, steep hills, and the wide ocean. Because St. Vincent is an island, it is surrounded by water.

The houses are bright orange, green, yellow, and blue.
She sees different animals: chickens, goats, sheep, and
cows. She waves at the people walking on the road.

When Nia gets to Gran-Gran's house, she runs to her room and jumps on the bed. It's just the way she remembers. Fluffy, oh so fluffy!

Bind Us Together With LOVE

She turns to Gran-Gran, and asks, "Can we go to the beach?"
"Sure, Sweet Love, let me pack a basket and we can head out."

While Gran-Gran packs a basket of her favorite snacks-cheese sandwiches, corn curls, coconut sugar cake, and Red Ju-c soda- Nia puts on her swimsuit.

The beach is beautiful! Clear blue water and hot sand. Some beaches on the island even have black sand. While Gran-Gran relaxes on the beach, Nia plays in the water for hours before she settles down to eat her snacks.

She says, "Gran-Gran, I am so happy to be here with you. I love you."

Gran-Gran says, "Sweet Love, these are precious moments that we have together. I wouldn't trade it for the world. I love you, too."

Gran-Gran and Nia hug each other and watch the beautiful sunset.

When Nia and Gran-Gran get home from the beach, there is sand everywhere! Nia takes a shower and puts on her nightie and head-tie and gets ready for bed. Before they go to sleep, Gran-Gran and Nia say a prayer.

"Good night, Gran-Gran.
I love you."

"Good night, Sweet Love.
I love you, too."

Outside her bedroom window, the stars shine against the black blue sky as the crickets sing lullabies.

"Kack-a-doodle-doo!" The roosters are the first to get up and they make sure the entire island is awake.

Today, Gran-Gran plans to go to the market to get food to cook for the family gathering. Nia is all set to leave when Gran-Gran stops her.

"Come and get something hot on your chest," Gran-Gran tells Nia.

She means Nia should drink something warm like tea or Milo before leaving home. Nia loves apple juice, but here on the island, they always have something hot to drink for breakfast.

When they get to the market, Nia is amazed.

"In New York, the markets don't look like this!" she exclaims.

There are fruits, vegetables, and crafts. Music is playing, and people are dancing. Others are talking and greeting each other. Women are carrying baskets filled with fruit on their heads. Gran-Gran buys chicken and fish. Nia gets a basket and picks up bananas, guavas, plums, plantains, okra, and callaloo.

As soon as they get home, they wash their hands and head to the kitchen. Gran-Gran does most of the cooking while sharing stories about life in St. Vincent, family traditions like praying before every meal and before bed every night, and family recipes. Gran-Gran makes cooking look so easy! She makes Nia's favorite dishes, bakes desserts, and squeezes fresh juice.

The relatives begin to arrive, and Nia meets her cousin, Halei, for the first time. She is about the same age, and they play dominoes. Each family carries a yummy dish to share. Pelau, fried bakes, stew chicken, provision, corn pie, callaloo soup, and breadfruit, just to name a few. There is more than enough food to eat! Surrounded by family, Nia's heart is filled with joy. They dance to sweet Soca music, laugh, and eat until they are all full.

The elders share stories about the past, and the children listen to learn more about their African, Garifuna, and Caribbean heritage. Generations of love surround them.

On Sunday, the family wakes up early in the morning to get ready for church. Gran-Gran combs Nia's hair into two perfect braids. She wears her favorite dress, shiny shoes, and straw hat to match.

Nia prays for her friends and family near and far. "God, thank you for this day. Thank you for family, friends, shelter, food, and clothing. Amen."

Nia is grateful for Gran-Gran, and wants to do something special for her. She wants to make banana fritters but for some reason she can't figure out the recipe!

But Nia is good at making peanut butter and jelly sandwiches. She prepares one for Gran-Gran, and also brews her favorite ginger tea. Everything looks perfect. She can't wait to see the surprised look on Gran-Gran's face! Nia also writes a letter and places it on the table.

She writes:

Gran-Gran,

Thank you for all that you do for our family. I am so happy I get to spend the summer with you and learn more about our beautiful island. You are kind, loving, patient, and beautiful in so many ways. I am grateful to call you my Gran-Gran, and I will always be your Sweet Love.

Love,

Nia

The summer days go by very quickly, and Nia's time on the island comes to an end. She wishes summer vacation would last forever. With every visit, Nia learns something new about her family, and even herself.

"I wish I could pack the island into my suitcase," says Nia as she packs her belongings. She does her best to fit everything – spices, candy, t-shirts, key chains, postcards, food, juice, and sea shells – into her suitcase.

In the morning, before Nia leaves for the airport, she gives Gran-Gran the tightest hug ever. Gran-Gran always gives the best hugs.

So long to the island that I love –
The Beaches
The Sunset
Family and Love
The Beautiful Hills
My Family.

As the plane climbs high up into the sky, returning to the big city, Nia thinks, "Even though I live in the big city, my home will forever be on the small island of St. Vincent."

66343600R00020